BREAKING UP

From Heartache to Happiness in 48 Pages
Written and Illustrated by Yolanda Nave

Workman Publishing, New York

Library of Congress Cataloging in Publication Data
Nave, Yolanda.   Breaking up.
1. Separation (Psychology) — Anecdotes, facetiae, satire, etc. I. Title.
PN6231.S495N38   1985   741.5′973 84- 40680
ISBN 0-89480-839-7

Workman Publishing Company, Inc.
708 Broadway
New York, New York 10003

Manufactured in Hong Kong
First printing March 1985
10 9 8 7 6 5

The End

Being alone is one thing.

Being *left* alone is another.

As soon as you're told you're no longer wanted or loved . . .

your self-image takes a turn for the worse,

and you begin to hurt.

You feel inept, inadequate . . .

and positively good-for-nothing.

However—with some effort—you can make yourself smile.

To show there are no hard feelings, help him pack his belongings.

Begin with his laundry. You want to be sure he has clean undies.
(Don't forget to starch them well.)

As you pack his socks, keep one from each pair. (Purely for sentimental reasons, of course.)

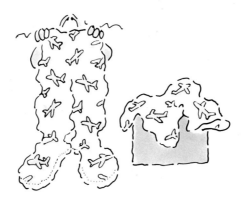

Make sure he has his favorite pajamas . . .

and anything else he can't do without.

Give him half of everything.

Then say good-bye . . .

And don't look back.

Even though there are some things you can't do alone . . .

Count your blessings!

Notice how the seat isn't left up anymore . . .

and how there's never any question about *who* ate the last chocolate chip cookie.

Enjoy your newly acquired wardrobe space...

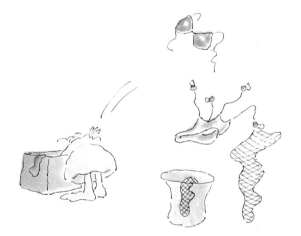

and while you're at it, get rid of those silly things he expected you to wear.

Do your weekly grocery shopping. Notice that your bill—like your appetite—is next to nothing

. . . and delight in the fact that two *can't* live as cheaply as one.

When whatsisname comes by to say he's sorry, agree with him—

and tell him no, you haven't seen his mother's picture, his magazine collection, or his favorite cashmere sweater.

Call all his friends you could never stand but had to tolerate, and tell them what you think of them!

Exercise your independence!

Weigh yourself.
You're getting closer to zero every day. Smile.

Upon retiring, wear the ugliest, most unsexy, sloppy, wonderfully cozy, snug flannel nightgown you own. . .

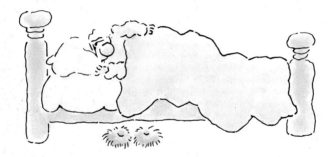

Go to bed with dirty teeth.

If sleeping alone isn't your idea of a good time . . .

one way or another, you'll adjust.

Time doesn't fly when you're not having fun.

But that's what time is for...
to make things heal, make things better.

Soon, you'll see that for every problem . . .

there is a solution.

And by and by, that old feeling called "loneliness" . . .

begins to feel like something called "freedom."